Starting Point for
RECOVERY

a simple 12-step guide for use in counseling for addiction recovery

DAVID ZAILER

CADCII, LAADC, CSAC
with Operation Integrity

STARTING POINT FOR RECOVERY
A Simple 12-Step Guide for Use in Counseling

© 2018 David Zailer

ISBN   978-0-692-07173-1
9 780692 071731

Published by:
Homecoming Books for Operation Integrity
24040 Camino del Avion Suite A115
Monarch Beach, CA 92629

Printed in the United States of America

Edited by Patty Kennedy

Cover Art by Ellie O'Connor

All rights reserved. No part of this publication may be reproduced, stored in a retrieval system, or transmitted in any form or by any means — for example, electronic, photocopy, recording — without the prior written permission of the publisher. The only exception is brief quotations in printed reviews.

All references to The Twelve Steps of Alcoholics Anonymous have been reprinted with the permission of Alcoholics Anonymous World Services, Inc. Referencing and reprinting AA quotes does not infer that Alcoholics Anonymous is affiliated with Operation Integrity or any other organization. AA is a program for alcoholism only, and considers itself a spiritual program of action and not a religious organization or mental health institution or facility. Thus, AA is not affiliated with any sect, denomination, specific religious belief or healthcare organization or facility.

Special thanks to the men and women of Operation Integrity and their families.

Welcome to the Adventure!

Contents

Introduction - Starting Point	9

Section One

Learning About Addiction	13
A Simpler Understanding of Addiction	14
How We Recover and Heal	14
Education - The Starting Point	15
Community - Environment for Recovery	16
Twelve-Step Community Resources	17
The Inside Work - Addressing Underlying Causes	18
The Healing Path - Action Steps to Healing	19
Personal Recovery Program Worksheet	20

Section Two

The History and Use of 12-Steps	23
The 12-Steps and The Serenity Prayer	24
Overview of 12-Step Principles	25

Section Three

Step One	27
Step Two	31
Step Three	37
Step Four	41
Step Five	45
Step Six	49
Step Seven	53
Step Eight	57
Step Nine	61
Step Ten	65
Step Eleven	69
Step Twelve	73

Introduction - Starting Point

No one wants to get addicted to something. We never asked to get addicted, we never wanted to get addicted, and we sure never meant for "it" (whatever it was we became addicted to) to take hold of us the way it has. It is fair to say, getting addicted to anything was the furthest thing from our mind. Nevertheless, addiction has become a destructive and painful part of life for many of us — skewing our decision-making, impairing our ability to function, literally robbing from us the freedom and dignity to live our lives the way we should. Along with the loss of freedom we experience, the out of control nature of addiction fosters deep feelings of isolation and loneliness, like we are *the only one* who struggles the way we do. And yet, we are not alone in our struggle. Everyone is addicted in one way or another.

Even with the loss of control related to our addictions, we are always responsible for our life choices. Recognizing our need for help is more difficult because of addiction, but the power to choose is never taken from us completely. Accepting help is our choice to make — get help and recover, or not. Only we can choose to begin the work of recovery; no one can make this decision for us. In choosing to get help we take the first step, moving ourselves forward in the simple process of making this decision.

Whatever games are played with us,
we must play no games with ourselves.
But deal in our privacy with the last honesty and truth.
 - Ralph Waldo Emerson

Counseling and/or psychotherapy is an invaluable part of a successful recovery effort. But often, the initial weeks in counseling/therapy are spent getting to know one another — counselor and client — developing the necessary comfort level and rapport that enables us to be honest with our counselor/therapist, and even with ourselves. The purpose of this short book is to introduce you to a personal 12-Step experience and blend it with your counseling/therapeutic opportunity. Sincere 12-Step work brings clarity and insight which — when shared with your counselor/therapist — helps them help you, increasing the effectiveness of your time with them. Combining a personal 12-Step program with counseling is a powerful one-two punch, blending two well-known, well-proven healing methods together for your health and well-being.

The following pages contain brief introductions to each of the 12 Steps. What you will find here is brief considering the material produced by Alcoholics Anonymous (AA) and the many 12-Step programs that have evolved from the success of AA. Please make full use of this book, but also look beyond it to the 12-Step Program materials for more depth.

You will also find questions for reflection. These questions are designed to help you be more connected with your thoughts and emotions. Think of your responses as journaling. You can use the space provided or use a supplemental notebook or journal, whichever is most helpful to you. Journaling will help you view and document your life experience in ways you may never have fully realized before, bringing your heart and mind together in a cohesive, connected, integrated way. Then, when sharing your journaling with your counselor, sponsor, or other helpful people, you will become more connected relationally with the world as a whole.

In addition to a 12-Step guide, I will do my best to inform you about the basic nature of addiction. No simple task! You will also find a section guiding you toward relationships that support your recovery, and a section encouraging you to address underlying issues that lead to addictive behavior. Finally, throughout this book, you will be gently and persistently encouraged to open your heart and mind spiritually. Spiritual revolution is at the heart and soul of recovery. I pray you find this if you haven't already.

~ David Zailer

Section One

LEARNING ABOUT ADDICTION & RECOVERY

Addiction is a clinical term referring to physiological and psychological dependencies that exhibit themselves in destructive behavioral patterns. **The American Society of Addiction Medicine (ASAM)** defines addiction in this way:

> Addiction is a primary, chronic disease of brain reward, motivation, memory and related circuitry. Dysfunction in these circuits leads to characteristic biological, psychological, social and spiritual manifestations. This is reflected in an individual pathologically pursuing reward and/or relief by substance use and other behaviors. Addiction is characterized by inability to consistently abstain, impairment in behavioral control, and craving, diminished recognition of significant problems with one's behavior and interpersonal relationships, and a dysfunctional emotional response. Like other chronic diseases, addiction often involves cycles of relapse and remission. Without treatment or engagement in recovery activities, addiction is progressive and can result in disability and premature death.

A SIMPLER UNDERSTAND OF ADDICTION

In layman's terms: *Addiction is a destructive relationship with any mood or mind-altering substance or experience that inhibits a person's freedom to live well.* It is a widespread human phenomenon where psychological, sociological and spiritual patterns of thinking and belief result in unhealthy damaging behaviors and physical dependencies.

Addictive behavior is characterized by negative consequences for us and even for our family and friends. It is further *characterized by a general loss of freedom* in our circumstances (negative consequences) and by flawed thinking and reasoning (cognitive distortions) reflected in our struggle to make clear and healthy choices and decisions. Addiction can be called the most human of all diseases or conditions, and no one is immune.

Addiction is a relational disorder in which obsession to things and experiences overrides the value of human relationships and personal responsibilities. Denial of this reality is at the core of our problems. We are often oblivious to damage caused by our most troubling addictions.

HOW WE RECOVER AND HEAL

Addiction may be defined clinically as a disease or disorder. In matters of religious faith, it may be defined as a condition of personal sin.

Each perspective has merit from that viewpoint. And both are true when seen inclusively. But, however it is defined, *addiction is never an excuse to continue destructive hurtful behavior.* We all are responsible for our behavior and for making the most of the information available and the opportunities to grow and change. *A diagnosis of addiction is a call to this responsibility, and taking responsibility is our first move toward recovery.* Coming to terms with how we are addicted is a call to action. It is a call to accept and apply a treatment plan and program, just as we would reasonably do with any other health issue. Furthermore, recognizing addiction calls for a change in our point of view — to accept expectations for change, embrace accountability and make full use of *all* available opportunities to heal, for our own well-being and for our loved ones.

EDUCATION - THE STARTING POINT

Education brings insight and understanding. It helps overcome confusion. It dispels stigma and shame. And it builds a foundation for compassion leading toward healing of our damaged relationships. Education guides our focus, directing us to helpful and appropriate resources and prioritizing our efforts for best results. Education is important for our families and loved ones too, helping them recognize the sadness and sickness of our condition. It will also help our loved ones establish healthy boundaries, so they are best equipped to deal with us personally and our behaviors objectively. The 12-Step programs have excellent simply worded literature to help inform you about specific addictions. You can find this literature at 12-Step meetings. Also, The American Society of Addiction Medicine has excellent information available online, www.asam.org.

HELPFUL BOOKS

Addiction & Grace	Dr. Gerald May
Addictive Thinking & Personality	Dr. Craig Nakken
Codependent No More	Melody Beattie

COMMUNITY - ENVIRONMENT FOR RECOVERY

While addiction is clinically assessed in behavioral terms, we must understand it as a profoundly relational disorder. Our addictions show that we came to value a "thing" (whatever it is) over people, so we must be willing to reverse course from our skewed (addicted) values and priorities, intentionally moving back toward honest living relationships with people, including our self and our God — all of which are essential to healthy community.

Community is the environment where healing grows organically and interpersonally for individuals and families. *An effective community for recovery is an environment of empathy, a place where people share common addictions and problems leading to an intuitive understanding of one another and finding a common solution and recovery together.* It's as if we can trade experiential and emotional shoes with one another in our recovery community, and they would fit with sufficient comfort to successfully walk our recovery journey together. And it is a journey, one that does not happen alone! Interpersonal insights grow in community. We see more clearly where we need to go and what we need to change to experience long-term successful recovery.

Twelve-Step communities are historically the most successful and available communities where we can invest ourselves, putting our roots deep into the lives of other recovering people whose shared experience will guide and nourish our own growth in recovery. But they are not the only places we can find community. Churches are becoming more aware of the reality of addiction, even developing their own faith-based recovery programs that are growing in popularity and effectiveness. There are also volunteer and service organizations, and even sports programs now designed to help people recover from addiction. Information for these various resources are easily located online.

TWELVE-STEP COMMUNITY RESOURCES

Alcoholics Anonymous	aa.org
Al-Anon & Alateen Family Groups	al-anon.org
Debtors Anonymous	debtorsanonymous.org
Gamblers Anonymous	gamblersanonymous.org
Sex & Love Addicts Anonymous	slaafws.org
Incest Survivors Anonymous	siawso.org
Adult Children of Alcoholics	adultchildren.org
National Clearinghouse on Alcohol	samsha.gov
Narcotics Anonymous	na.org
Emotions Anonymous	emotionsanonymous.org
Overeaters Anonymous	oa.org
Anorexics/Bulimics Anonymous	aba12steps.org
Codependents of Sex Addicts	cosa-recovery.org
Codependents Anonymous	coda.org
Marijuana Anonymous	marijuana-anonymous.org
Pills Anonymous	pillsanonymous.org
Nicotine Anonymous	nicotine-anonymous.org
Workaholics Anonymous	workaholics-anonymous.org

THE INSIDE WORK - ADDRESSING UNDERLYING CAUSES

Our intrapersonal world is the not-so-obvious center point of our life. We live from emotional, psychological and spiritual places within us. The reality of our interior life is revealed in how we live our lives day in and day out. Yes, our addictions are physical and behavioral problems. But our 12-Step work helps us see how the pain and problems of our inner world instigate and compel us addictively in our outer world.

So, we must *address the underlying issues that contribute to our addictive behavior*. These may include but are not limited to: abuse or abandonment; depression; unprocessed grief; abusive religious training; narcissism or living under the spell of a narcissist; toxic shame; poorly managed stress; loneliness or feeling alienated; boredom; unresolved anger; unhealthy relationships; a family history of addiction.

Section One

THE HEALING PATH - ACTION STEPS TO HEALING

The "how to" of addiction recovery is well-known and simple. Basic action steps are as follows:

- Involvement in a 12-Step fellowship, attending as often as possible.

- Individual 12-Step work with a sponsor. Following the guidance of a mentor, developing a relational lifestyle often referred to as *A Spiritual Program of Action*.

- Family involvement in the recovery process through Al-Anon or a similar recovery fellowship that addresses codependency and/or co-addiction.

- Meet with a qualified therapist or counselor. Include family in therapy as suggested by counselor.

- Identify triggers and underlying causes. For example, there may be an unhealthy excessive need for affirmation, family of origin issues, childhood abuse or abandonment, unhealed grief, an unhealthy view of God which may even exist in those who have religious training and church experience, other addictions, mental illness, mood disorders.

- Identify and address all addictions such as overeating, alcohol and other drugs (yes, alcohol is a drug), gambling, unhealthy relationships, unhealthy religious activity, use of pornography, sexual addictions, and others.

PERSONAL RECOVERY PROGRAM WORKSHEET

This worksheet is to help identify essential relationships and activities for recovery. It is designed around 12-Step recovery groups along with other peer support and professional resources.

My name (first name only if you prefer):

_____

My addictive problem is:

_____

      Twelve-Step meetings are the building blocks of recovery — in our meetings we will find the environment for help and healing. Attending 90 meetings in 90 Days has consistently proven effective. Guides to meeting schedules can be obtained online and at meetings – write your schedule below.

Monday: Saturday:

Tuesday: Sunday:

Wednesday:

Thursday:

Friday:

Getting a sponsor is key in recovery. This person should be someone you respect and who will hold you accountable for meeting attendance and 12-Step work. Someone who will be honest with you, encourage you, and help you stay focused.

Name and phone of my sponsor/mentor:

_____

Obtaining help from experts and professionals is a helpful part of recovery, one we should utilize whenever possible. Consult your doctor or insurance provider as necessary.

Name and phone of my counselor/therapist:

_____

Name and phone of my doctor/psychiatrist:

_____

Names of recovery partners:

_____

Section Two

HISTORY AND USE OF THE 12-STEPS

The 12-Step process was developed by Alcoholics Anonymous in the 1930s to help men and women recover from alcohol addiction. The process has been so effective 12-Step Programs have been applied with success to countless areas of human struggle, helping people from all cultural and religious backgrounds.

A personal 12-Step program is not an exact formula, but more a strategic pathway for intrapersonal growth and relational healing. It is most effective when applied with an open heart and mind. *Working the steps*, as the recovery saying goes, helps connect us with the often unseen reality of our lives. It helps us gain a truer understanding of our past *and* our present, which is the first step in changing the direction of our future. Our own addicted life, when brought into the revealing light of the 12 Steps, will speak wisdom to us from the reality of our self-destructiveness. Not just that we are alcoholics, drug addicts, food addicts, sex addicts, gamblers or porn addicts (or any other label that may apply), but more to the entangled disagreements of our heart and mind. Gaining a truer perspective of how splintered we have become in our addicted lives is the first step in becoming a healthy, balanced, whole person.

For more information on the history of the 12 Steps, read *Alcoholics Anonymous Comes of Age* from Alcoholics Anonymous World Services.

THE TWELVE STEPS

Adapted from Alcoholics Anonymous

Step One	We admitted we were powerless over our addictions, that our lives had become unmanageable.
Step Two	We came to believe that a Power greater than ourselves could restore us to sanity.
Step Three	We made a decision to turn our will and our lives over to the care of God as we understood Him.
Step Four	We made a searching and fearless moral inventory of ourselves.
Step Five	We admitted to God, to ourselves, and to another human being the exact nature of our lives.
Step Six	We became entirely ready to have God remove all these defects of character.
Step Seven	We humbly asked Him to remove our shortcomings.
Step Eight	We made a list of all persons we had harmed, and became willing to make amends to them all.
Step Nine	We made direct amends to such people wherever possible, except when to do so would injure them or others.
Step Ten	We continued to take personal inventory and when we were wrong, promptly admitted it.
Step Eleven	We sought through prayer and meditation to improve our conscious contact with God as we understood Him, praying only for the knowledge of His will for us and the power to carry that out.
Step Twelve	Having had a spiritual awakening as the result of these steps, we tried to carry the message to others, and to practice these principles in all our affairs.

OVERVIEW OF THE 12-STEPS PRINCIPLES

Steps 1-3 bring a change of perspective — a shift in our thinking that resets our value system and priorities. Essentially this: *I can't do it; but I believe God can do it; I will trust and let God do it.*

Step One	Honesty & Acceptance
Step Two	Hope & Faith
Step Three	Faith & Trust

Steps 4-9 are action steps that bring personal clarity and promote healing in our relationships spiritually (connection with God), interpersonally (connection with our self) and with other people.

Step Four	Courage
Step Five	Relational Honesty & Integrity
Step Six	Desire & Willingness to Change
Step Seven	Spiritual Humility
Step Eight	Social & Relational Responsibility
Step Nine	Personal Responsibility & Justice

Steps 10-12 are about ongoing growth where we incorporate every aspect of our lives into our recovery work, intentionally setting selfishness aside in the interest of helping others, which happens to be the best thing we can do for ourselves.

Step Ten	Perseverance
Step Eleven	Spiritual Awareness & Growth
Step Twelve	Transformation, Service & Diligence

Serenity Prayer

God, grant me the Serenity to accept the things I cannot change,
Courage to change the things I can,
and Wisdom to know the difference.

Section Three

STEP ONE - We admitted we were powerless over our addiction, that our life had become unmanageable.

Step One is an experience of overriding deep personal failure because we have failed to get our addictions under control. It is hitting bottom physically, emotionally, spiritually, or maybe even all three. In Step One, we admit that our addictions are stronger than we are. We admit our sense of personal power — our ego — is conquered. We recognize this reality: *Staying the same with our addictions is more painful and difficult than the pain and fear we feel about changing our lives and ourselves.*

Having been blinded by denial in the past, perhaps the thing most difficult for us to accept is the increasing destructiveness of our addictions. Not recognizing this now will probably make things worse for us because of the progressive nature of addiction. One thing is for sure, our "bottom" can always go deeper, right up until we die. Step One calls us to surrender a fight we have been losing all along. Our surrender must be done with full conviction of heart and mind if our efforts to recover are to be successful.

The power of Step One is a paradox. In admitting we are powerless over our addictions and cannot presently manage our own lives, we become open to look for and accept help to heal our addictions and guide us to a better life going forward.

STEP ONE - REFLECTIONS

Describe your addiction(s) as you understand it/them.

Write about your experiences related to your addiction(s).

Describe how your addiction(s) have hurt you and how you feel about this.

Describe your experience of failing to stop your addiction.

Describe negative consequences you have experienced due to your addiction — professionally, relationally, financially, to your health, or to your reputation.

How do you feel about yourself before, during, and after you have acted out in your addiction?

What do you think and feel when you consider sharing this journaling with your counselor, sponsor, or someone in your recovery group?

Step One - INSIDE-OUT ACTION STEP

Spend time reading over and pondering what you wrote in your Inner World Reflections for Step One. Don't correct or delete anything. Let it simply be what you wrote down. Share it all with your counselor and your sponsor.

Step Two - We came to believe that a Power greater than ourselves could restore us to sanity.

Step Two is an outgrowth of Step One — with a natural desire to live, we move instinctively, sometimes even desperately, from hopelessness toward hope. Step One points us to see our desperation, connecting us with the reality of our emptiness, our sadness and our hopelessness. And yet, when we get honest about our addicted condition and simply hope for a better life than what we have had in the past, we will naturally — like a child does when afraid — reach out and take hold of the help needed to stop the downward spiral of our lives.

Step Two honors our most sincere hope and desire. It is about recognizing new ways of thinking and living and seeing new ways to succeed where we have failed. *We come to believe* and understand there is a solution for every problem, and these solutions will present themselves to us when we're open-minded enough to look for and receive them.

Step Two is not about religion or church, although religion and church may play a role for some of us. Step Two is about a personal faith and trust — learning to accept help, knowing where to go and whom to ask for help, and trusting in the help that comes our way.

There are lots of higher powers. Our 12-Step meeting can be a higher power. Some individuals like our sponsor, counselor, or doctor may function as a higher power. Of course, God is the ultimate Higher Power. The key for us is our willingness to go for help and accept and trust the help that is available, surrendering the tendency to be our own higher power, our own "god." Learning to relate to God/Higher Power — whoever we understand Him to be — and other people in a personal trusting way is key to utilizing the resources that will empower long-term recovery.

It is essential we understand that trusting in God — whoever we understand God to be — is impossible until we see how we try to play God ourselves, usually without even realizing it. This same principle of effective trust applies to our ability to trust others, too. You must recognize that you cannot solve your problems on your own. You must be willing to accept help and trust other people and God.

Step One clarifies our need for help, making Step Two an essential shift in our perspective. We have to be willing to let go of our addictions. This includes matters related to money, sex, career, hobbies, food, medications, chemicals, relationships and unhealthy social interests. If you are unable or unwilling to surrender your addictions now, you can move in that direction by honestly admitting your reluctance to your sponsor, counselor and others in your recovery meetings. Recovery is possible only when we are honest.

Step Two - REFLECTIONS

What do you feel when you think of asking for help?

How do you feel when you think of trusting other people to help you succeed where you have failed on your own.

Describe both your thoughts and feelings about God, and getting help from God.

How would you describe God, or your Higher Power?

What do you need God to do for you that you cannot do for yourself?

What do you think and feel when you read "restored to sanity?"

What do you think and feel when you consider sharing this journaling with your counselor, sponsor, or someone in your recovery group?

Step Two - INSIDE-OUT ACTION STEP

Spend time considering what you wrote in your Inner World Reflections for Step Two. Don't correct or delete anything. Share with your sponsor and counselor struggles you feel about trusting God and other people.

Step Three - We made a decision to turn our will and our life over to the care of God as we understood Him.

Considering the desperation we admit in Step One and the hope we realize in Step Two, the most reasonable thing for us to do is to decide that God, as we understand Him to be, will guide and direct our lives going forward. This is not a religious decision, but a supremely practical decision; God must be more than a religious conversation piece if He is going to be anything for us at all. However we understand God, we must accept Him as our ultimate Higher Power, the absolute Essential and Source for all that is good and helpful in our life. This means that we turn everything over to Him: our will, our life, our recovery, our families, our relationships, our career, even little things like a broken-down car or appliance.

In Step Three, we make God the center of our focus rather than ourselves. We are no more important and no less important than anyone else and, above all, we understand that our God is the essential starting point for everything good in life. The key to Step Three is willingness, which we must exercise every day, while honestly admitting any struggles we face in making our decision to trust in the God of our understanding. Remember this: no matter how far we move forward, recovery progresses only as we admit we are not in control and that we need help and guidance from God and other people.

Step Three is where we decide who we will become in life and what our life will be like from here on out. Many find that Step Three is where the miracle in recovery begins.

ABOUT GOD

Moving our concept of God from religious to personal is the most important thing we do in recovery. This is not to suggest that anyone's religious view of God is in any way inferior, but until someone's relationship with God is personal, no amount of religious profession or activity will give us the needed power to overcome our addictions.

Seek to find the God of your understanding to be One who is loving, caring, and greater than anyone or anything. We don't have to be religious to accept this idea, although most but not all religions teach this to be the nature of God. *The point is that we open our minds and our hearts to believe in the love and care of God, and to live and act accordingly.*

STEP THREE - REFLECTIONS

What have you thought of God in the past personally, not theologically or religiously?

Section Three

Are you willing to have a new idea of God?

How do you feel about trusting in the God of your understanding?

What do you need God to be for you?

What do you feel when you think of surrendering outcomes, no longer being solely responsible for everything?

What do you think and feel when you consider sharing this journaling with your counselor, sponsor, or someone in your recovery group?

Step Three - INSIDE-OUT ACTION STEP

Consider what you wrote in your Inner World Reflections for Step Three. Relax, and let go of pain you may have experienced from hurtful religious experience. Embrace your experience as worthwhile. Share what you wrote with your counselor and your sponsor.

STEP FOUR - We made a searching and fearless moral inventory of ourselves.

Steps One, Two and Three are discoveries and decisions made internally that will influence the direction of our lives. Some people reach basic sobriety from these first three steps, but others may not. Long-term recovery requires action, and Step Four is about taking action. Step Four marks a shift in our recovery work. We shift our focus from our inner world, our attitude and perspective, to a work of courageous action. This kind of action will ultimately bring healing to our relationships with ourselves, with our God, and with important people in our lives.

We face ourselves objectively in Step Four. We own up honestly to the consequences of our choices in life, seeing — perhaps for the first time — how we have manipulated others and ourselves. This may be a frightening endeavor, but we will find courage as we admit our fear to the God of our understanding, our sponsor, and our counselor, and then move forward in spite of the fear we feel. Courage never exists in the absence of fear. Only when feeling fear will we learn what it means to act with courage and move in the very direction in which we are afraid.

Step Four is your *response-ability* as a partner in the new life God will give you. No one can do Step Four for you. You must do it yourself, allowing your Higher Power/God to use it for good in your life going forward.

Step Four - REFLECTIONS

(You may want to use an additional notebook or journal.)

Write your family history and your reflections on your family.

Write your history and reflections related to your sexual/romantic history.

Write your history and reflect on your current financial condition.

Section Three 43

Write your history and thoughts related to your educational and career history.

Write your thoughts related to your religious and spiritual history.

What do you think and feel when you consider sharing this journaling with your counselor, sponsor, or someone in our recovery group?

STEP FOUR - INSIDE-OUT ACTION STEP

Read over your Inner World Reflections for Step Four. Realize the courage you show when writing about your life and personal history. Embrace your effort with appreciation. Share what you wrote with your counselor and your sponsor.

STEP FIVE - Admitted to God, to ourselves, and to another human being the exact nature of our wrongs.

Step Five may feel like the most challenging thing we've faced so far in recovery, but moving forward in this experience, we will likely find it to be the most rewarding. Our addictions increased our sense of shame, isolating us spiritually and relationally from other people, which increased the likelihood we would act out. The action of Step Five interrupts this isolating downward spiral, turning us toward healthier relationships with the God of our understanding and important caring people we have in our lives.

In Step Five, we'll disclose and even discuss what we came to know about ourselves in our Step Four inventory. We'll take what we learned, laying it all out on the table and talking it over with the God of our understanding and another person. We won't hide or change anything. We'll just let God and someone else see our life for what it has been and see us for who we are — all of it, the good and the bad. We no longer have reason to run or hide or make excuses. We'll be honest about how we've created many of the problems we face today. We will accept responsibility for our life as a whole, even some of the problems we didn't directly create. For most of us, this will be the first time the honest reality of our lives will be received with respect and appreciation.

The practice of telling one's story and having it heard and validated is proven to heal people emotionally, spiritually, and even neurologically, reversing years of isolation and abuse, even healing entrenched negative thinking and believing. Step Five gives us the opportunity to become healthier, happier and better-connected members of the relational world we live in.

STEP FIVE - REFLECTIONS

After reflecting on your Step Four inventory, write out the basic observations you see about your life.

What new awareness do you realize after reading over your Step Four inventory?

What do you need to share with another person?

What burden or secret do you need to let go of?

Name a few people you would like to share what you discovered in Step Four.

What do you think and feel when you consider sharing this journaling with your counselor, sponsor, or someone in your recovery group?

Step Five - INSIDE-OUT ACTION STEP

Spend time reading over and pondering what you wrote in your Inner World Reflections for Step Four. Embrace the reality of your life experience as you would accept anyone else's life experience. Share what you wrote with your counselor and your sponsor.

STEP SIX - We became entirely ready to have God remove all these defects of character.

Step Six is not about *doing* anything. It is about *becoming* — becoming ready to experience and respond to life in healthier ways than we have in the past. While not the active hands-on work of Steps Four and Five, Step Six is not passive; it requires a decisive commitment of the will. It is giving up who and what we think we are and letting go of our demands and expectations about how we think things should be. In Step Six we become ready to have our basic character renewed and changed, and grow into a different kind of person than we have been in the past.

Remember, in Step Three we made a decision to turn our will and our life over to the care of God as we understand Him. With this decision in mind, we are *response-able* for living in such a way that God is able to make changes in us. Living differently — in faith (trust coupled with good actions) — the process of change happens inside of us beginning with the way we value ourselves, our God, and the people in our lives. We must be willing to let go of our expectations, especially expectations about the various aspects of life that are beyond our control. This change in our values helps us respond in a more content and caring way in the future.

STEP SIX - REFLECTIONS

Write about your experience from doing Step Five, sharing with another person the exact nature of your wrongs.

Describe any pain you have experienced because of the character flaws you see in yourself.

How have your character flaws added to your problems?

Do you want a healthier inner-world that will help you make better decisions and actions? If so, write your thoughts related to this.

What do you think and feel when you consider sharing this journaling with your counselor, sponsor, or someone in your recovery group?

STEP SIX - INSIDE-OUT ACTION STEP

Ponder the character defects that have kept you from living your best life. Share with your sponsor and counselor what you realize, and what changes you want to make in the way you think and live.

STEP SEVEN - We humbly asked Him to remove our shortcomings.

A successful long-term recovery program is built on humility. With this in mind, it is important we have a clear understanding of what humility is. Humility as it relates to recovery can be defined as a realistic understanding of who we are and how we relate with the God of our understanding and the people around us. Above all, humility is a deep commitment to interpersonal truth. Humility means we examine our thoughts, our feelings, and our actions to keep a healthy and balanced self-awareness, especially as it relates to others. This builds integrity into the way we think and act. Humility helps us see ourselves honestly, to see where we have made mistakes and how we can live better going forward. Humility helps us interact freely with the God of our understanding and other people on all levels. Humility is the key to experiencing the spiritual power of God in personal and practical ways.

Step Seven is a request born of humility. It comes from a growing confidence in our God, a balanced appreciation for others, and a sincere conviction that we cannot solve our character problems by ourselves. In Step Seven, we humbly ask the God of our understanding to do for us what we cannot do for ourselves.

STEP SEVEN - REFLECTIONS

Principles in *The Seven Step Prayer* from Alcoholics Anonymous are fundamental to a sustainable recovery program.

My Creator, I am now willing that You should have all of me, good and bad. I pray that You now remove from me every single defect of character which stands in the way of my usefulness to You and my fellows. Grant me strength, as I go out from here, to do Your bidding. Amen.

What part of the Step Seven Prayer stands out most to you?

How have you previously denied yourself the power of the Step Seven Prayer?

What do you think and feel when you consider sharing this journaling with your counselor, sponsor, or someone in your recovery group?

Step Seven - INSIDE-OUT ACTION STEP

Write your own personal version of the Step Seven Prayer. Don't copy, write your own. And share what you wrote with your counselor and your sponsor.

STEP EIGHT - We made of list of all persons we had harmed, and became willing to make amends to them all.

To move toward recovery and build a healthy future, we must recognize and take responsibility for any harm we have done to other people. Step Eight is an exercise that helps heal the relationships damaged by our addictive behaviors and self-centeredness, so that we can be *response-able* and move beyond the negative relational consequences we've brought on ourselves.

Step Eight assumes and implies that we carry hidden within us a burden of guilt and shame for virtually every incident where we have hurt or rejected or ignored the need of others. Step Eight is an opportunity to begin setting right the wrongs we have done, lightening the burden of guilt and shame we have carried alone for too long. Remembering when others were hurt because of our self-centeredness creates painful and shameful feelings — feelings we so want to avoid but can't. By making a list of people we harmed and how we harmed them, we bring our shame to a place where we can do something about it. Our memories no longer need to be like ghosts terrifying us inside. Our memories can be reformatted into valuable experience that teaches and guides us in the future.

The work of Step Eight continues the shame-reducing process we began in Step Four and Step Five. Simply admitting our wrongdoing and shortcomings is not enough in the relational and reciprocal world we live in. We must be specific in how we have affected the lives of others and be willing to make things right wherever possible. Otherwise we will continue living in the isolation that fuels our addictions. Isolation kills people.

STEP SEVEN - REFLECTIONS

List the name of any person you think or feel has been negatively affected by your addiction and self-centeredness.

Person			Reason

List any reason why you are unwilling to make things right with any of the people you listed.

Are you willing to become willing?

What do you think and feel when you consider sharing this journaling with your counselor, sponsor, or someone in your recovery group?

STEP EIGHT - INSIDE-OUT ACTION STEP

Look over the list of names you wrote and inventory your thoughts and feelings. Share what you wrote and what you think and feel with your counselor and your sponsor.

Step Nine - We made direct amends to such people wherever possible, except when to do so would injure them or others.

Step Nine is an effective proven way for us to move past old hurts toward healthier relationships and a healthier life. It may seem as if Step Nine is a one-sided experience because we are the ones who take the initiative, but it is not one-sided at all. Everyone — beginning with us — benefits when we make amends for our wrongs.

Step Nine is about opportunities and possibilities, not guarantees. Our job is to simply make good use of the opportunities before us. When we do this, it becomes possible for our fractured and broken relationships to be healed, to become new and possibly even better than ever before. At the same time, it is important that we recognize we may never be able to repair all of the damage and hurts we have caused. We also need to understand that apologies alone will never be enough to make things right. We cannot earn our way back into the lives of others with empty promises. Most of us have tried that many times with no success. We must remember that we are not in control of the results. There are no guarantees. The only thing we control is our attitude and our actions. We can only do what we can do.

Step Nine - REFLECTIONS

With the list of people you made in your Step Eight Reflections, what can you do at this time to make things right?

What can or should be done later to make things right?

What cannot be done because it may harm others?

How can you make living amends to those to whom you cannot make direct amends?

Step Nine - INSIDE-OUT ACTION STEP

Share what you wrote with your counselor and your sponsor.

STEP TEN - We continued to take personal inventory and when we were wrong, promptly admitted it.

Step Ten marks a shift in our recovery program. It is the first of what we can consider — along with Steps Eleven and Twelve — steps of ongoing growth or, perhaps, maintenance steps. This is where we move past the heavy lifting of Steps Four through Nine and toward an ongoing way of life that will enable us to heal and grow long term throughout our lives.

Step Ten is about ongoing day-to-day habits, a lifestyle where we continually monitor our thoughts, feelings, and actions so we will quickly see if or when we slip away from God's purpose and plan for our lives. Step Ten is about vigilance. It is about making consistent changes that keep our lives balanced and healthy.

Step Ten is about more than just staying "sober," although staying away from our past addictions will always be an essential concern. This step is about being healthy and balanced so we can reliably bring goodness to the people God brings our way. Honest self-searching must be a regular, disciplined part of our day if we are going to make the most of our lives. Until we are willing to consistently recognize and admit the wrongs that still lurk within us, and unless we persistently make healthy changes in our thinking and living, we will not experience the joy life has to offer, nor will we have the persistence to bring goodness to others, which is the way we experience happiness in the most joy-filled way.

STEP TEN - REFLECTIONS

What do you now see that hurts your relationship with God or people?

What do you feel guilty or ashamed about?

Write your thoughts about continuing to take inventory.

What do you think and feel when you consider sharing this journaling with your counselor, sponsor, or someone in your recovery group?

Step Ten - INSIDE-OUT ACTION STEP

Share what you realized and wrote with your counselor and your sponsor.

Step Eleven - Sought through prayer and meditation to improve our conscious contact with God as we understood Him, praying only for the knowledge of His will for us and the power to carry that out.

Built into us is the instinct to search for and find things we need and want to make life safer and more comfortable. We do it naturally and instinctively in most every area of our lives. We search for the best bargains at the mall, we look for the best food for our families, we research information related to politics, healthcare, investments, and education. Even our addictions show how we have — in destructive ways usually without realizing it — sought comfort and safe refuge from the painful futility that plagued our heart and mind. Above everything else, we have been searching for a meaningful connection that will satisfy us at the most intimate and personal level.

Step Eleven is a practice that helps us focus our efforts in recovery, putting to good use our instinct to search. It helps us learn more about and be closer to the God of our understanding, and to have our hearts, minds, and lives molded for goodness by God. Step Eleven is not necessarily a religious activity, although it may be for some. It's more like meeting a friend for coffee, an evening conversation, or an intimate encounter with our loved one — the God of our understanding. This is because our relationship with God, just like all other relationships, requires that we actively engage the one we want to be close to. Step Eleven brings spontaneity and continuity to our relationship with God, making it intimate and personal and forever. As we begin to relate with God in these ways, we will learn to enjoy Him, and we'll want to be with Him often and always.

STEP ELEVEN - REFLECTIONS

God knows our every thought and feeling. How do you feel when you consider this?

Prayer is the practice of speaking our mind and heart to God. What do you want to say to God?

What do your actions express that you may not realize you are saying to God?

Meditation is the practice of listening to God. How do you feel about dedicating time to be quiet and listen to the God of your understanding?

Step Eleven - INSIDE-OUT ACTION STEP

Spend 1-2 hours alone with God, with only your journal or notepad to write your reflections and new revelations that come to you. Share what you experience in this time with your counselor and your sponsor.

STEP TWELVE - Having had a spiritual awakening as the result of these Steps, we tried to carry the message to others, and to practice these principles in all our affairs.

We began our journey because we needed to heal an addiction. And while healing has begun, other things may happen that we did not expect. We are seeing things from a healthier, more honest viewpoint. Our relationships are improving. And, perhaps best of all, we are experiencing the gift of ongoing, intrapersonal transformation.

The transformation the God of our understanding gives us is limitless in its positive effects when we surrender and seek relationship with Him. He changes and improves us in every important way. We used to hide in shame, but now we feel blessed when other people want to get to know us. We realize there is no reason for us to hide ourselves away anymore. We can now see how our addictions are like deadly storms in the ocean — they motivate us to seek the safe harbor of our God and the fellowship of other recovering people. As we set our moorings deep into our God, we are transformed into powerful lovers of people. This is the essence of the spiritual awakening.

Just like we would enthusiastically tell others about our favorite restaurant, the movie we enjoyed, or our children or grandchildren, we have good reason to share our life experiences with others in hope that our recovery experience will encourage them. Nothing holds us back when we humbly walk with our God and serve others with care and kindness.

Going forward, our work is similar but also expanded from when we first started our recovery journey, continuing to apply 12-Step principles to our lives, to walk with our God, and help others do the same.

STEP TWELVE - REFLECTIONS

What new discoveries have you made from doing this 12-Step work?

How would you describe your spiritual condition now as opposed to when you first began?

What do you want to share with others about your experience?

Section Three

Who are the people you would like to tell your story to?

What things do you now see that hinder your growth, your happiness, and your ability to relate with God and others in healthy ways?

What do you need to do now to further your recovery?

STEP TWELVE - INSIDE-OUT ACTION STEP

Spend time reading over and pondering what you wrote in your Inner World Reflections for Step Twelve. Share what you wrote with your counselor and your sponsor.

Section Three

Notes

Notes

Notes

More Books by David Zailer and Operation Integrity

www.operationintegrity.org

OPERATION INTEGRITY

www.ingramcontent.com/pod-product-compliance
Lightning Source LLC
Chambersburg PA
CBHW051956290426
44110CB00015B/2268